Learning to Read, Step by Step!

 Ready to Read **Preschool–Kindergarten**
• big type and easy words • rhyme and rhythm • picture clues
For children who know the alphabet and are eager to begin reading.

 Reading with Help **Preschool–Grade 1**
• basic vocabulary • short sentences • simple stories
For children who recognize familiar words and sound out new words with help.

 Reading on Your Own **Grades 1–3**
• engaging characters • easy-to-follow plots • popular topics
For children who are ready to read on their own.

 Reading Paragraphs **Grades 2–3**
• challenging vocabulary • short paragraphs • exciting stories
For newly independent readers who read simple sentences with confidence.

 Ready for Chapters **Grades 2–4**
• chapters • longer paragraphs • full-color art
For children who want to take the plunge into chapter books but still like colorful pictures.

STEP INTO READING® is designed to give every child a successful reading experience. The grade levels are only guides; children will progress through the steps at their own speed, developing confidence in their reading.

Remember, a lifetime love of reading starts with a single step!

For Kali, our creature pal forever

*The editors would like to thank Jim Breheny, Director Bronx Zoo and EVP of WCS Zoos &
Aquarium, New York, for his assistance in the preparation of this book.*

Visit us on the Web!
StepIntoReading.com
randomhousekids.com

Educators and librarians, for a variety of teaching tools, visit us at
RHTeachersLibrarians.com

ISBN 978-0-553-52472-7 (trade) — ISBN 978-0-553-52473-4 (lib. bdg.) —
ISBN 978-0-553-52474-1 (ebook)

Printed in the United States of America
17 16 15

STEP INTO READING®

2

STEP

READING WITH HELP

A SCIENCE READER

Wild Predators

by Martin Kratt and Chris Kratt

Random House 🏠 New York

Predators can be strong, fast, and smart.

They can have sharp teeth and claws or other amazing Creature Powers.

But what are predators?

Predators are animals
that catch and eat
other animals.

The animals that
predators catch
are called prey.

But catching prey
can be tricky. . . .

Get ready to activate
Predator Powers with us,
the Wild Kratts!

Jaguars!

Jaguars are big jungle cats that are powerful swimmers. These cats can catch caimans!

They can be black or spotted.

Ospreys!

Ospreys have big eyes
to spot fish in the water.
When an osprey
sees a fish,
the bird dives
and plucks the fish
out of the water
with sharp talons.

"My turn. Biggest fish wins!" says Chris.

Mouse Lemurs!

Not all predators look fierce.

The mouse lemur looks cute!

"My new fuzzy friend!"

says Martin.

Don't be fooled!

Mouse lemurs are fierce.

They can jump far and

grab insects and lizards

in their paws.

"Run!" the Kratts shout.

Fossas!

Fossas live and hunt
on the island
of Madagascar.
Fossas have incredible
climbing powers.

They can run down
a tree headfirst!
Their favorite prey
is lemurs.

Polar Bears!

Polar bears hunt on land and in the sea.

Their white fur hides them while they hunt in the snow.

This is called camouflage.

Polar bears are strong
swimmers.
They hunt seals and walrus
in the icy waters
of the Arctic Ocean!

Black-Footed Ferrets!

Black-footed ferrets are long, slim, and fast.

They run through tunnels
to catch their favorite prey—
prairie dogs!

Praying Mantis!

A praying mantis has
two long front legs
with spikes.
When a bug walks by,
the praying mantis
snatches it up!

"Let me try!" says Martin.

"Don't bug me, bro!"

Chris says.

Cheetahs!

Cheetahs are the fastest land predators. They chase speedy prey like gazelles.

Cheetahs can run seventy
miles per hour.
Cheetahs are long
and skinny,
which helps them sprint.

Wolves!

Wolves are also runners.
They can run
for a long time.

Wolves hunt in a pack.
They work together
to catch big animals,
such as moose.

Thorny Devils!

Ants are the thorny devil's favorite prey.

In fact, ants are the only thing this reptile eats!

A thorny devil
uses its sticky tongue
to pick up ants.
It can eat over a thousand
ants each day!

Roadrunners!

Roadrunners are the fastest-running birds in North America. They chase and catch lizards and other small desert creatures.

These quick birds also hunt
venomous rattlesnakes.
"Too much tug-of-war
for me," says Martin.
"Time to activate
Roadrunner Powers!"

"Race you to our next meal!" says Chris.

"You're on!" says Martin.

Go, Creature Powers!